At the Forge of Liberty

Other Books by Alden R. Carter

—————————— **Alden R. Carter** ——————————

☆ **AT THE FORGE OF LIBERTY** ☆

Franklin Watts
New York/London/Toronto
Sydney/1988
A First Book

Library of Congress Cataloging-in-Publication Data

Carter, Alden R.
At the forge of liberty.

(A First Book)
Bibliography: p.
Includes index.
Summary: Presents an overview of the Revolutionary
War, discussing causes, campaigns, and leaders.
1. United States—History—Revolution, 1775–1783—
Juvenile literature. [1. United States—History—
Revolution, 1775–1783] I. Title. II. Series.
E208.C33   1988   973.3   88-5626
ISBN 0-531-10569-5

For Hawthorne and Trevelyan Beyer:
citizens of two great nations

Contents

Chapter 1
The Struggle for Philadelphia
11

Chapter 2
New Allies, New Hope
25

Chapter 3
The Far-flung War
39

Chapter 4
Raiders by Land and Sea
48

Chapter 5
Disaster in the South
56

Chapter 6
The Amazing Campaign
72

Chapter 7
The Tide Turns
89

Suggested Reading *92*

Index *93*

Many thanks to all who helped with *At the Forge of Liberty,* particularly my editor, Marjory Kline; my mother, Hilda Carter Fletcher; and my friends Don Beyer, Dean Markwardt, Sue Babcock, and Georgette Frazer. As always, my wife, Carol, deserves much of the credit.

★ 1 ★

─────────── The Struggle for ─────────── Philadelphia

The pound of drums and the shrill of fifes came faintly on the August morning. A buzz of excitement swept the crowd gathering on the Philadelphia street. The Continental army—George Washington's army—was coming. John Adams surveyed the crowd and smiled grimly. A few months before, many of these same Philadelphians had expected to greet a different army, the mighty British and German legions of General Sir William Howe.

Unlike Adams's Boston, Philadelphia had been a city of divided loyalties since the beginning of the American Revolution in 1775. Now, two desperate years later, Washington intended to throw a scare into the Loyalists and inspire the patriots of America's largest city.

Even Adams—the most optimistic of patriots—had often doubted that this day would ever come. He remembered well all the dark days when the Revolution had seemed on the point of collapse. That the American cause had survived—had even grown healthy—was something of a miracle.

The Accidental War

The American Revolution had begun almost by accident in April 1775. It was a war almost no one really wanted. Most Americans had long felt a deep loyalty to the British Empire. Until the early 1760s, Britain had treated the thirteen colonies fairly. The colonists had governed most aspects of their lives and prospered under the protection of the mother country's army and navy.

During the French and Indian War (1754–1763)—called the Seven Years' War in Europe—colonial militiamen had fought alongside regular British soldiers against the French. Together, they had driven the French from North America and made the British Empire the most powerful on earth. The colonists expected to share in the benefits of victory. Instead, the British king and government decided to curb the independence of the colonies. The British legislature, Parliament, closed the recently won lands to colonial settlement and passed new taxes and laws to regulate colonial trade. British troops were stationed in America to help enforce Parliament's policies.

Parliament's actions raised a storm of protest in America. Britain had never granted the colonies the right to elect representatives to Parliament, and "No taxation without representation" became the colonial slogan. When the colonists refused to pay taxes or buy British goods, Parliament passed even harsher measures. For a decade, the colonists and the British government argued. Each new round of taxes and protests further soured the relationship between mother country and colonies.

Boston became the scene of the most violent protests. The British government responded by closing the port and placing the city under military rule in the spring of 1774. Furious, the people of Massachusetts began preparing to fight the British army. Alarmed by the deepening crisis in Massachusetts, twelve of the colonies sent representatives to Philadelphia for the First Continental Congress. The delegates debated the future of America, then wrote to the king, asking him to find a peaceful solution to the conflict between Britain and the American colonies. The king refused to listen.

The hope for peace ended in the spring of 1775. A force of British regulars from Boston set out to capture patriot leaders and military supplies. On the morning of April 19, 1775, the British soldiers confronted American militia in the village of Lexington. A single—probably accidental—shot started the Revolution.

Against the Odds

Those first days of the Revolution now seemed long ago to Adams. Overnight, Congress had been thrust into acting as a national government. It created the Continental army and named Washington commander in chief. Washington's army forced the British to abandon Boston without a fight in the spring of 1776. That July, Congress approved the Declaration of Independence.

Britain had no intention of letting its prized colonies break free. That same July, the British struck at New York City with an army of thirty-two thousand, the largest army ever sent from British shores. It included thousands of German mercenaries, soldiers hired to fight for Britain. The British commander, General Sir William Howe, nearly destroyed Washington's army in the fighting around New York. Howe's second-in-command, Lord Charles Cornwallis, chased Washington across New Jersey.

Early in the winter of 1776, Howe's great army camped less than forty miles from Philadelphia. Only the icy Delaware River and a few thousand starving and exhausted continentals lay be-

Philadelphia in 1777 was America's largest city.
Here, citizens gather outside the Old State House.

tween Howe and the American capital. To the hoots and jeers of the Loyalists, the Continental Congress fled the city. Even John Adams felt that the Revolution was nearly over.

Then, with a crushing victory nearly in his grasp, General Howe decided to delay his attack until spring. He scattered his troops in outposts, then returned to New York City for a season of parties. Washington made him pay dearly for that strange decision. In two daring—almost suicidal—attacks, the Continental army crossed the Delaware to smash Howe's garrisons at Trenton and Princeton, New Jersey. In its darkest hour, the Revolution had been saved.

Sixteen Thousand Strong

The steady rhythm of thousands of marching feet roused Adams from his memories. He turned his attention back to the sunlit Philadelphia street as the long column came into view. His heart swelled with pride and hope. The army had grown by leaps in the spring and summer. In March, it had numbered fewer than three thousand men. Now, on July 24, 1777, it had sixteen thousand.

At the head of the army rode George Washington—tall, unsmiling, almost forbiddingly dignified. Two years in command had aged Washington, hardening the line of his jaw and deepening the shadows beneath his cold, blue-gray eyes. His amateur army had suffered defeat after defeat. Time and again, it had escaped complete destruction by only the thinnest of margins. Ragged and starving, the army had slogged on through suffering that would have crushed a professional European army. And every setback, every agonizing march, seemed to leave Washington more upright, more stern and soldierly than ever.

Watching the general, Adams felt a twist of envy. He had always wanted to be a soldier. But at forty-two and "pigeon-plump," he was poor material for the hardships of war. Fate had given him other duties. Washington raised his sword in salute. John Adams, delegate to the Continental Congress and chairman of the Board of War, bowed solemnly in reply.

Marching in ranks twelve deep, the soldiers took two hours to pass. Most of the men still lacked the training, uniforms, and much of the equipment of professional soldiers. Yet, their enthusiasm and numbers impressed. Adams later wrote his beloved wife, Abigail, "[They were] extremely well armed, pretty well clothed and tolerably disciplined." He was hopeful that the late summer of 1777 would bring American victories.

Preserving the Army

Washington also had high hopes. Still, he had long realized that his main duty lay in preserving the army. Without it, the Revolution would collapse. He could risk battle only when the chances of success were high. He had spent the spring and early summer of 1777 in southern New Jersey, holding the high ground that overlooked the road from New York City to the Delaware and, beyond it, Philadelphia. Several times Howe had tried to lure him down from the heights, but each time Washington had refused combat.

The American soldiers did not lack courage. In defensive positions, they fought as well as any army. However, they lacked the training to move and fight in tight ranks on open ground. The British and German regulars were masters of rapid maneuver and the devastating bayonet charge. Few American regiments had the discipline or even enough bayonets to match them.

Washington's tactics had left Howe in a maddening predicament. He could not afford the bloody cost of attacking uphill against the American positions. Nor could he march to the Delaware for a crossing while Washington hovered in his rear, ready to strike when the British army was most exposed. In frustration, Howe had withdrawn to New York City to plan another way to "bag the fox."

Howe Sets Sail

Late in July 1777, Howe had embarked most of his army on a fleet of 260 ships and set sail. Washington was left guessing where he had gone. Howe might sail into the open ocean, arrange his fleet in the best order, then return to sail past the city and up the Hudson River. Far to the north, General John Burgoyne was leading a powerful British force south from Canada to invade the Hudson River Valley. If Howe and Burgoyne joined forces, they could field an army of overwhelming power. Or, Howe might be bound for the Delaware, where his fleet could sail up the river to within fifteen miles of Philadelphia. Or, perhaps Howe was headed for Charleston, South Carolina, the most important port in the southern colonies. Washington badly needed to know.

As it turned out, Howe still had his eye on Philadelphia. Rejecting the shorter but more hazardous route up the Delaware, he sailed for Chesapeake Bay. On July 22, Washington received news that the British fleet had been sighted making for Head of Elk (today's Elkton), Maryland. Washington assembled his troops and began the march south from New Jersey. The men were in good spirits, much heartened by the news that General John Stark had wiped out a large detachment of Burgoyne's force at Bennington, Vermont.

On July 24, Washington paraded his troops through Philadelphia to the joy of John Adams and the city's patriots—and the discomfort of the Loyalists. The army moved on to camp near Wilmington, Delaware. From this position, Washington hoped to block Howe's advance on Philadelphia. The need for defensive tactics irked Washington. He loved the assault, longed to strike at Howe often and hard. Yet, two years of bitter experience had taught Washington patience. He would preserve the army at all costs—even the loss of Philadelphia.

Brandywine

Howe's army rested from the rugged sea voyage until September 2, when it began the fifty-mile march to Philadelphia. Washington kept his army a few miles distant while his scouting parties ambushed any British soldiers unwise enough to stray from Howe's column. On September 10, Howe reached the wooded banks of Brandywine Creek and found the American army strung out along the far shore to oppose a crossing.

Washington had placed the strength of his army at Chad's Ford under the command of his best field general, Nathanael Greene. A mile upstream, General John Sullivan guarded Brinton's Ford with another strong force. Further upstream, smaller American units covered other crossing points.

Howe chose a daring tactic. He ordered General William Knyphausen, the commander of Howe's German mercenaries, to hold the attention of the Americans at Chad's Ford. Meanwhile, Howe and Cornwallis would lead the main part of the army upstream until it could cross unopposed. They would circle back to surprise the Americans from the rear. The tactic was not without its dangers. If the Americans discovered that Howe had divided his army, they could destroy Knyphausen, then wheel

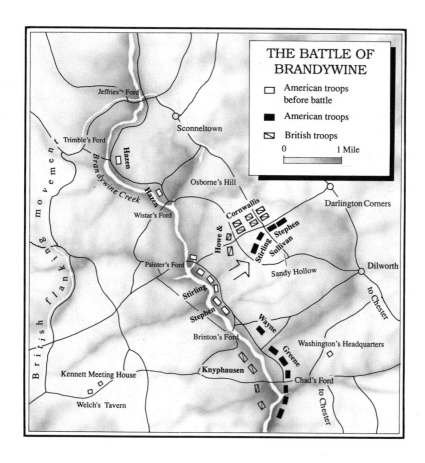

THE BATTLE OF
BRANDYWINE

□ American troops
before battle

■ American troops

◨ British troops

0   1 Mile

Jeffries' Ford

Trimble's Ford

Sconneltown

Hazen

Brandywine Creek

Hazen

Osborne's Hill

Wistar's Ford

Cornwallis

Darlington Corners

Howe & Knyphausen

Stirling

Stephen

Sullivan

Dilworth

Painter's Ford

Sandy Hollow

Stirling

Stephen

Wayne

to Chester

Brinton's Ford

Washington's Headquarters

Kennett Meeting House

Knyphausen

Greene

Chad's Ford

Welch's Tavern

to Chester

British flanking movement

to face Howe. Yet, Howe was confident that Washington's cau-
tion would give the British time to complete the maneuver.

Howe got his troops on the road at 4:00 A.M. on September
11. In midmorning, Knyphausen started a fierce artillery duel
with the Americans at Chad's Ford. Washington received con-
flicting reports about Howe's movements. He hesitated. Meanwhile, Howe's force crossed the Brandywine unopposed and
circled back to get behind the American lines. About 2:30 P.M.,

the British emerged from the woods and paused to rest on Osborne's Hill, barely two miles behind Sullivan's positions near Brinton's Ford. Alerted by a breathless dispatch rider, Washington sent orders directing Sullivan to swing his force away from the stream to face Howe.

Confident in the superiority of his troops, Howe took his time readying an attack. Sullivan's men rushed to new positions along a low ridge a mile and a half from Osborne's Hill. At 4:00 P.M., Howe attacked. The British regiments smashed through the gaps left in Sullivan's hastily formed lines. The American left and right wings collapsed. In the center, three thousand Americans fought desperately against twice their number. Five times they were forced back, five times they charged to regain the lost ground. At last, they broke under the pressure.

Complete disaster threatened, as the American retreat turned into a stampede. Then Sullivan's men met one of Greene's brigades hurrying to the battle. Led by Washington and Greene, the brigade had covered four blistering miles in forty-five minutes. Greene's men opened ranks to let the retreating troops through to re-form. Greene's brigade began a slow, dogged withdrawal under intense British fire. The British attack lost momentum. The Americans made a stand in a narrow valley called Sandy Hollow. As darkness fell, they turned back charge after charge by crack British grenadiers, the pride of the king's infantry.

The Americans at Chad's Ford were also in retreat. Knyphausen had attacked across the Brandywine when he heard the battle begin to the north. The Americans under General Anthony Wayne met the Germans with heavy musket and cannon fire. In the close quarters, the cannon fired grapeshot—the terrible canisters filled with musket balls. The waters of the Brandywine turned red as the two armies struggled. Neither

*Cornwallis leads the light infantry
into battle at Brandywine.*

side held the advantage until a force of Howe's grenadiers stumbled from the woods to the north. The grenadiers had lost their way chasing some of Sullivan's men. By chance, they were now in a perfect position to "roll up" Wayne's right flank. The grenadiers attacked, forcing Wayne's entire force to retreat. But American discipline held. At each fence, grove, and house, the Americans turned to deliver another punishing volley. As daylight faded, Knyphausen ordered his troops to break off the pursuit.

Retreat in the Night

All through the hot night, the tired Americans trudged away from the scene of another defeat. The fighting had broken up most of the regiments, and the army was little more than a mob. Yet, spirits remained surprisingly high. No wounded man lacked a friendly arm to help him along. The regional jealousies that had plagued the army disappeared as men from different colonies encouraged each other. An officer reported that he frequently heard the words, "Come, boys, we shall do better another time."

Twelve miles from the battlefield, the road crossed Chester Creek. At the bridge, the young Marquis de Lafayette, a French volunteer on Washington's staff, halted the retreat. His officers sorted out the men and counted casualties. Washington and Greene arrived to take charge. In the dawn, the mob became an army again.

Philadelphia

Brandywine had cost the Americans roughly twelve hundred dead, wounded, and captured—twice the British losses. By any standard, Howe had won a brilliant victory. Yet, to Howe's disgust, Washington refused to take to the hills. Instead, he again positioned the Continental army between the British and Philadelphia. For two weeks, the armies marched and countermarched. Small detachments fought hot fights. On September 21, a British force surprised fifteen hundred Americans under General Wayne near Paoli Tavern. In a savage night attack, the British inflicted some three hundred casualties with only slight loss to themselves. Exaggerated stories of the "Paoli Massacre" enraged the colonies and brought new recruits to Washington's army.

Tired of fencing with Washington, Howe decided to outmaneuver him once and for all. He marched toward Reading Furnace, a village where Washington had stored most of his military supplies. Washington moved hastily to defend the stores. Howe rapidly changed direction, crossed the Schuylkill River, and marched into Philadelphia without opposition on September 26, 1777.

Washington's dogged defense of Philadelphia had not been entirely wasted. The British captured the city too late to do great damage to the American cause. The previous winter, when the Continental army had dwindled to a few thousand starving scarecrows, the loss of Philadelphia might well have destroyed American morale and ended the war. But in the fall of 1777, Washington's army was growing in spirit, skill, and numbers.

America shrugged off the loss of Philadelphia as it had the earlier losses of New York City and Newport, Rhode Island. Philadelphia had not been a true capital housing large government agencies processing mountains of paperwork. The Continental Congress could carry on its business from almost anywhere. (In its lifetime, it would move nine times.) Nor had Philadelphia been essential to the commercial health of America. Boston, Charleston, Savannah, and a dozen other cities thrived despite the efforts of the British navy to blockade America's ports.

Even more important, rural America with its farms, country villages, and small towns remained almost entirely outside British control. The British effort to put down the Revolution had collided with the immensity of America. The British could capture city after city, but rural America would continue to feed and man Washington's army.

★ 2 ★

New Allies, New Hopes

In late September 1777, news of American victories in the North more than balanced the loss of Philadelphia. General Horatio Gates had trapped a large British invasion force in upstate New York and was on the brink of destroying it.

The British invasion had begun early that summer. General John Burgoyne led an army of some eight thousand British and German soldiers south from Canada in an attempt to take the Hudson River Valley and split the New England and Middle Atlantic colonies. He pushed the Americans from Lake Champlain, then marched overland to the Hudson. Sharp battles and the long march through the wilderness took a toll on his army. North of Albany, Burgoyne found his way blocked by Gates and a rapidly growing American army.

With Gates was the fiery Benedict Arnold, perhaps the best field general in the American army. On September 19, Arnold led his men in a savage fight at Freeman's Farm. Only Gates's failure to reinforce Arnold at the critical moment prevented a great victory. After the battle, the two generals argued so violently that Gates relieved Arnold of his command.

The armies watched each other as Gates gathered reinforcements and Burgoyne waited in vain for a British march up the Hudson from New York City. On October 7, another battle erupted. Against orders, Arnold charged into the fighting. The American troops followed him in a series of wild assaults that broke through the British defenses. Burgoyne was forced to withdraw in the night following the battle of Bemis Heights. Surrounded on the heights of Saratoga, he surrendered his remaining fifty-eight hundred troops on October 17, 1777.

Germantown

In Pennsylvania, Washington's men heard the news of the battle of Freeman's Farm soon after the British capture of Philadelphia. They were already in a fighting mood, eager to revenge Brandywine and the Paoli Massacre. No one wanted another battle more than Washington, and he felt that his army was finally strong enough to go on the offensive.

Howe had camped the largest part of his army—some nine thousand men—at Germantown, five miles north of Philadelphia. Washington devised a complicated plan to overrun the British camp. Four separate American columns would march through the night, then hit the camp from all sides at dawn. Washington would accompany General John Sullivan at the head of the largest column.

The plan looked brilliant on paper but proved nearly impossible to carry out. Rough, winding roads slowed the marching columns. Daybreak on October 4 found only Sullivan's column in position outside Germantown. In a thick fog, the Americans stormed into the west side of the camp. The British regulars formed quickly to meet the attack. They fought with all their famed skill and courage, but the Americans pushed

PENNSYLVANIA-
NEW JERSEY
CAMPAIGNS 1777-78

American advance

American retreat

British advance

British retreat

▲ Battle

0   20 Miles

Washington 1777
Washington 1778
to White Plains
Hudson River
New York City
Long I.
Bound Brook
Staten I.
New Brunswick
Raritan River
Hopewell
Kingston
Princeton
Englishtown
Monmouth
Jun 28, 1778
Reading Furnace
Whitemarsh
Clinton 1778
Allentown
Valley
Forge
Schuylkill River
Germantown
Oct 4, 1777
Brandywine Creek
Paoli Sept 21, 1777
Philadelphia Sept 26, 1777
Ft. Mifflin
PENN.
Brandywine
Sept 11, 1777
Ft. Mercer
Nov 20, 1778
NEW JERSEY
Howe 1777
Howe
Delaware River
MD.
Head of Elk
Chesapeake Bay   DEL.

them toward the center of the camp. A second American column, under General Nathanael Greene, reached Germantown forty-five minutes late and launched an attack from the north.

For a short time, it looked as if the Americans were about to win the most important victory of the war. However, the fog made coordination almost impossible. Regiments of the two American columns collided and fired on each other. The other two prongs of the American attack failed to appear. On the west, five companies of British regulars retreated to stout Chew House and poured a withering fire on the Americans from behind its stone walls. As the American advance slowed, Howe rallied his men and led them in a strong counterattack.

In the fog, the noise of battle seemed to come from all sides. Inexperienced American troops became confused. Were they winning or about to be surrounded? They began retreating. More and more regiments gave way under the British counterattack. Four hundred men of an American regiment that refused to retreat were surrounded and forced to surrender. Washington, Greene, and other officers braved hot British fire in attempts to stem the retreat. It was hopeless. The soldiers were exhausted by the long hours of battle after the hard night march. Even those with fight still left had run short of ammunition.

Washington recognized that he must organize the best retreat possible—a task he had performed all too many times before. He did not let his worn-out men rest until late afternoon, when they had reached a safe camp twenty-four miles from the battleground.

The Americans had suffered another defeat, with nearly eleven hundred men killed, wounded, or captured against about half as many on the British side. Yet, it had been an extremely impressive effort. In size and ambition, the attack had exceeded any American plan of the war. Washington's troops had fought bravely and, despite the flaws in the plan and remarkably bad luck, very nearly delivered a crushing blow.

Winter Approaches

Through the rest of the autumn, the two armies kept a wary distance. Scouts and detachments hunting for supplies—a practice called foraging—fought skirmishes, but neither commander committed his troops to a major battle.

Howe worried about his supply lines. Washington controlled most of the countryside and could attack overland supply columns at will. On the Delaware, American forts blocked supplies from reaching Philadelphia by water. Howe ordered the forts taken. The American garrisons at Forts Mifflin and Mercer put up stiff resistance, but British and German infantry supported by Royal Navy ships cleared the Delaware by late November. Howe could rest easy until spring.

Washington faced a grim situation. The months of marching and fighting had begun to tell on his army. Clothes and boots had worn thin. Blankets, winter coats, and tents were in desperately short supply. Exhaustion and exposure led to illness. Many men dreamed of home as they counted the remaining days of their enlistments. Washington knew the signs. Nothing he could do would prevent thousands from heading home with the first snow. He must find winter quarters and preserve the remainder of his army until spring brought new recruits and returning veterans to the ranks.

Valley Forge

Washington's generals debated the choice of winter quarters. The temporary camp at White Marsh was dangerously close to Philadelphia, and several officers argued for a march to Wilmington, Delaware, where the army could pass a comfortable winter. However, a move to Wilmington would leave eastern Pennsylvania and much of New Jersey at Howe's mercy. General Anthony Wayne suggested Valley Forge, some eighteen miles northwest of Philadelphia. Washington took this unfortunate advice.

Valley Forge took its name from an iron forge that had once operated on the wooded plateau above the junction of Valley Creek and the Schuylkill River. The steep drops to the creek and river made the site easily defensible. However, the plateau provided little cover from the winter wind. Even worse, it stood in the middle of country already picked clean by the foraging parties of both armies.

On December 21, the army trudged into Valley Forge after an exhausting, week-long march through snow, rain, and sleet. Washington would later write: "You might have tracked the army from White Marsh to Valley Forge by the blood of their feet." It was the beginning of a long winter that would make the name Valley Forge a symbol of terrible suffering and great courage.

Dr. Franklin in Paris

While the Continental army froze and starved at Valley Forge, an old man in Paris was waging one of the most important campaigns of the war. Benjamin Franklin's skills as an inventor, scientist, writer, diplomat, and philosopher had made him America's most famous man. Since 1776, he had served as the senior American representative to France. Amid the glittering

Eighteen miles northwest of Philadelphia, Washington's army went into winter quarters at Valley Forge, today a symbol of terrible suffering and great courage.

life of the French court, Franklin cut a homely figure. Short and plump, he dressed plainly in black with a fur hat on his balding head. He was unfailingly good natured, modest, and polite. The nobility—particularly the women—loved to pamper the "good doctor."

Franklin's appearance and relaxed ways disguised his plotting to bring France into the war on the side of America. The cause of liberty aroused little sympathy in the French court. France had a strong monarchy that gave its citizens few of the rights America was fighting for. However, the French king and his ministers were interested in anything that would weaken the British Empire. France had lost its American possessions to Britain in the French and Indian War, and the rebellion of Britain's American colonies represented a chance for revenge.

Since 1776, France had been shipping arms to America in secret. Franklin wanted more than supplies. He wanted French soldiers and—even more important—the aid of the French navy. The French hesitated; open assistance would lead to war with Britain in Europe, America, and wherever the two great empires competed.

The events of the autumn of 1777 gave Franklin new arguments. American morale had not collapsed after the defeat at Brandywine or the loss of Philadelphia. The narrow defeat at Germantown demonstrated that the Continental army could not only take blows, but hit and hit hard. Most important of all, the British surrender at Saratoga had shown that the Americans could win major victories. France would not be investing in a lost cause, but in an infant nation that every day grew stronger and more dedicated to its independence.

The news of Saratoga tipped the balance. In February 1778, the French and American representatives signed an alliance. Both parties pledged to wage war until Britain granted American in-

Benjamin Franklin at a reception at the French Court in 1778. Seated, are the king and queen, Louis XVI and Marie-Antoinette.

dependence and satisfied French claims in the Caribbean and Africa. An important clause assured the Americans that France would make no attempt to regain its possessions on the North American mainland. Franklin triumphantly forwarded the treaty to the Continental Congress for approval.

Misery at the Forge

In the bitter early months of 1778, no one at Valley Forge knew of Franklin's success in Paris. The men of the Continental army lived from day to day in near despair. On the windy plateau, outside duties were a freezing agony. Being inside one of the rough log barracks was barely more comfortable. Measuring fourteen by sixteen feet, each cabin housed twelve men. The soldiers slept on lice-infested straw beds or on the dirt floor itself. Heavy blankets and warm clothes were luxuries known to only a few. Meal after meal, the men had only firecake—a thin dough of flour and water—to cook over their smoky fires. In their weakened condition, many of the men fell sick. Talk of mutiny and desertion filled the cabins' dark corners.

Washington worked desperately to keep his army from falling apart. He got little help from the Continental Congress, which had never mastered the task of supplying the army. He asked Nathanael Greene to reorganize the army's supply and transportation system. Greene, who preferred battle to paperwork, accepted the responsibility unwillingly but carried it out with energy. He sent foraging parties far afield in search of supplies. On Washington's orders, civilians were paid fairly for whatever the army took.

By March, the army had begun to mend. Fewer than six thousand men remained, but they were at last receiving adequate food and clothing. Equally important, they had a new sense of purpose given them by a smiling, heavyset German officer, Frederick William Augustus Henry Ferdinand, Baron von Steuben.

Drillmaster

Steuben had presented himself to the Continental Congress as a former lieutenant general in the Prussian army. (Actually, he had been only a captain and his fancy name and noble title were pure invention.) Congress had listened to bragging soldiers of fortune before, but Steuben offered to serve the American cause without pay and in whatever capacity Washington would think best. Congress applauded his generosity and sent him to Valley Forge in February 1778.

Washington may have doubted some of Steuben's claims to former high rank, but he recognized the hearty German's ability. He appointed him acting inspector general in charge of training. Steuben quickly saw that the troops badly lacked the parade-ground practice necessary for large groups of men to move quickly on a battlefield. He did not even have to hear the veterans' stories to know that the army had lost many battles because it simply could not maneuver as well as the British.

Steuben spoke German and French but little English. He wrote a drill manual in French. Aides translated it into English and made hundreds of copies by hand. For the first time, all the regiments of the Continental army would be using the same system. Next Steuben formed a model company with men from every regiment of the army. Thousands of soldiers gathered to watch Steuben drill his company.

Steuben occasionally stumbled over the English drill commands, and his soldiers would go marching every which way while the red-faced Steuben cursed and bellowed in a mixture

Baron von Steuben drills the American soldiers at Valley Forge.

of German, French, and English. Fortunately, Steuben had a sense of humor and soon everyone would be laughing. A little comedy was a great blessing in that bleak winter.

By the end of March, Steuben had sent the men of his model company to help train the rest of the army. In a remarkably short time, the Continental army began to march, look, and feel like a professional army. Steuben added more maneuvers to the training and taught the men to load and fire in compact formations. For the first time, the army got regular training in the use of the bayonet.

Steuben, too, was getting an education. The independence of the Americans often frustrated him. He wrote to a friend, "[In Europe] you say to your soldier 'Do this' and he doeth it; but [here] I am obliged to say 'This is the reason why you ought to do that'; and then he does it." Yet, he was also coming to admire the American soldiers. He told Washington that no European army could have held together through the sufferings of Valley Forge. Steuben was convinced that such courage and a little elementary training would bring the army victory.

★ 3 ★

The Far-flung War

France declared war on Britain in the spring of 1778, drastically changing the character of the American Revolution. America became only one battleground in a struggle between two great empires competing in Europe, Africa, the Caribbean, India, and the Far East.

The British government recognized that much of the fighting against its old enemy would be done at sea, particularly in the Caribbean, where both nations had valuable possessions. More troops must be sent to garrison the Caribbean islands. For the time being, Britain could no longer afford large land operations in the thirteen colonies. The government ordered General Henry Clinton, who had relieved Howe, to evacuate Philadelphia and concentrate the British army in New York City.

Clinton had replaced Howe as commander of British forces in May. He was a careful and reliable soldier, although he lacked Howe's tactical brilliance. He prepared the evacuation of Philadelphia with his usual thoroughness. He loaded some of his supplies, the army's sick, and about three thousand Loyalists aboard ships and sent them down the Delaware. The remainder of the army—some ten thousand men—would march overland to New York City. An astonishing amount of equipment accompanied the army, including wheeled laundries, bakeries, hospitals, and blacksmith shops. No officer traveled without trunks of uniforms, books, and luxuries. Every common soldier had acquired possessions during his stay in Philadelphia. Hundreds of camp followers, mostly women and children, accompanied the army.

Early on the morning of June 18, Clinton got his army on the road. It crossed the Delaware that day and began a slow march through New Jersey. The supply train of fifteen hundred wagons stretched some twelve miles. In the first six days, the army covered only thirty-five miles.

Washington Marches

At Valley Forge, Washington had received news of the British evacuation well before Clinton's march began. He ordered small American detachments to shadow the British, while he led the main army on a route that would intercept Clinton. En route, his generals debated what should be done. The Continental army had grown to some 13,500 men. The troops were in excellent physical condition, well trained, and eager to fight. Greene, Wayne, Lafayette, and Steuben argued for an attack on Clinton's plodding army.

They were opposed by Washington's second-in-command, General Charles Lee. A professional soldier, Lee had served bravely in the British army during the Seven Years' War in Europe. Like many former British officers who had settled in America, he had backed the colonial cause at the outbreak of the Revolution. The largely amateur American officers, including Washington, were impressed by Lee's experience. Lee constantly played on their respect to undercut Washington. Lee despised the former militia colonel and thought himself far better suited for command of the army.

Through his own carelessness, Lee had been captured in December 1776. Years after his death, family members would reveal that Lee spent much of his time in captivity conspiring with General Howe against the colonial cause. However, Washington did not doubt Lee's loyalty when he agreed to exchange a captured British officer for Lee in April 1778. Lee rejoined the Continental army just in time to make serious trouble.

To Monmouth Court House

On June 27, Clinton's army rested at Monmouth Court House, near Freehold, New Jersey. Washington camped at Englishtown, five miles to the west. He informed his officers that he had decided to attack when circumstances looked favorable. Although Lee had argued against risking battle, Washington offered him command of the advance force. Lee at first declined, then accepted.

Early the next morning, scouts brought news that the British were again on the march. General Knyphausen and four thousand Germans led the column, followed by the long supply train, then four thousand British infantry under Clinton, and finally, a rear guard of two thousand elite grenadiers and light infantry under Cornwallis. Washington ordered Lee forward with five thousand men and instructions to attack using whatever tactics best suited the situation.

A mile north of Monmouth Court House, Lee's force made contact with the rear guard under Cornwallis. From the beginning the battle was a mess. Lee had no plan and made none when skirmishing began. With numbers overwhelmingly on the American side, his subordinates begged for an all-out attack. Instead, Lee pulled his right wing back, leaving his left dangerously exposed. Mystified by the move and Lee's failure to send orders, the commanders on the left pulled back. In a few minutes, all the American regiments were in retreat—much to the surprise of Cornwallis, who quickly organized a pursuit.

The unbeaten but thoroughly confused Americans retreated west along the hot, dusty road. They met Washington, riding ahead of the main force marching to support Lee. The general demanded to know why they were retreating. No one knew. Washington spurred forward until he found Lee. Barely able to control his anger, Washington snapped, "What's all this confusion for? And what is the cause of this retreat?" Lee delivered a fumbling answer, and Washington exploded. An aide would later say that Washington "swore till the leaves shook on the trees."

Little time could be wasted on swearing or explanations. Scouts brought word that Cornwallis had been reinforced by Clinton and was only fifteen minutes behind the retreating Americans. Washington rode through the retreating men, calling on them to take courage. Never had Washington seemed more commanding. Seeing their tall general on his great white horse, the men cheered and began forming a line.

Washington galloped forward with General Wayne. They came to the last of the retreating men, two regiments of Pennsylvania and Maryland continentals. Two hundred yards beyond them, Washington could see the pursuing line of redcoats. Wayne took charge of the continentals and began a dogged delaying action. Washington wheeled his horse and galloped to the rear to organize the main line.

The Americans formed along the west side of a swampy ravine spanned by a narrow bridge. General William Alexander,

The legendary Molly Pitcher reloading
a field cannon at the Battle of Monmouth

known as Lord Stirling for the ancient Scottish title he claimed, commanded the American left wing. General Greene commanded the right wing. On nearby Comb's Hill, Washington placed artillery and two regiments of infantry at right angles to Greene's wing. General Steuben watched with satisfaction as the American regiments moved into position with the precision of a parade-ground drill. Wayne's troops withdrew slowly under heavy fire to re-form behind a hedge in front of the American center.

Clinton Attacks

General Clinton thought the retreat had delivered the Continental army into his hands. He was soon to think differently. He hurled an attack against Stirling's wing. For an hour the fighting was ferocious, then two American regiments burst from the woods on Clinton's right and drove the British back.

Clinton assaulted the American right. Greene's troops and the artillery on Comb's Hill blunted the attack. Clinton threw infantry and cavalry against the American center, but Wayne's troops coolly poured grapeshot and massed musket fire down on them. The British fell back all along the line.

The British paused for an hour to rest. In late afternoon, grenadiers formed five hundred feet in front of Wayne's men. The Americans could hear the British colonel yell, "Forward to the charge, my brave grenadiers." A few months before, the sight of the charging pride of the British army would have panicked almost any American regiment. No longer. Wayne's men held their fire until the onrushing grenadiers were only forty yards away, then cut them down in rows.

One final time the British assaulted the center. This time

the mass of attackers forced Wayne's men to withdraw, but the main American line held. Exhausted, the British fell back.

The Reckoning

Washington wanted more than a defensive victory, but the hour was late and his men too exhausted for further action. In the morning, he found that Clinton had slipped away in the night. It was too late to overtake the British march to New York City.

The battle of Monmouth Court House was militarily a draw. Casualties were about even on both sides and remarkably light—less than 400 each—considering the heavy action. (An additional 576 British and German soldiers deserted during the march.) The Continental army had missed a chance for a great victory but had proved the value of the winter's training. Perhaps most important was the effect the battle had on the American commander in chief. Disgusted with General Lee, Washington began trusting his own judgment more.

Lee demanded a court-martial to clear his name. Washington obliged. The court found Lee guilty of disobeying orders and insubordination. He was suspended from command for a year. Unable to accept this sentence, he wrote angry letters to Congress and received word that his services would not be wanted in the future. His departure was a decided benefit to the army.

The French Arrive

On July 8, 1778, tall masts appeared on the horizon off the Delaware Capes. At long last the French had arrived. A fleet of twelve mighty ships of the line—the battleships of the day—

and numerous escort ships and transports sailed into American waters. The Comte d'Estaing commanded the fleet and the four thousand soldiers on board. He and Washington met to discuss strategy. A great opportunity lay before them. For the first time in the war, the British could be denied control of the seas. If d'Estaing could defeat the smaller fleet of Admiral Lord Richard Howe (General Howe's brother), then Washington could put the British in New York City under siege.

It was a good but difficult plan. Howe refused to weigh anchor and sail out of the protected waters of New York harbor. After eleven days of waiting, d'Estaing sailed north to try a similar strategy against the British garrison at Newport, Rhode Island.

General John Sullivan had assembled a force of ten thousand men at nearby Providence for the attack on Newport. The allies' plan quickly fell to pieces. Sullivan unintentionally insulted d'Estaing by landing his troops on Newport Island a few hours ahead of schedule. D'Estaing took the first excuse to sail for Boston where he could refit his ships. Left without naval support, Sullivan was forced to beat a quick retreat to the mainland. D'Estaing soon sailed for the Caribbean, his infantry still aboard, ending the first attempt at cooperation by the new allies.

Autumn Again

Through the late summer and fall, Washington's army camped at White Plains, near New York City. His men stayed alert for a move by Clinton's army, but it did not come. In October, the army received a large shipment of uniforms, mostly blue, from France. For the first time in the war, most of the army could be dressed in uniform—a major boost for morale.

In November, Washington's army went into winter quarters at Morristown, New Jersey. Few of the men facing yet another long winter would have guessed that the major action in the North was over for good. A few small battles would occur, but the deciding campaigns of the war would be fought in the South.

★ 4 ★

Raiders by Land and Sea

Far from the Revolution's main battlegrounds, hundreds of small, bitter fights raged. Loyalists fought patriots in every colony. On the frontier, Indians raided homesteads and white settlers burned Indian villages. At sea, American warships and armed merchant ships carried on a long, nasty campaign against the Royal Navy.

Coastal Raids

After France entered the war in 1778, the British abandoned large land operations in favor of hit-and-run raids along the coast. Connecticut was particularly hard hit. In July 1779, a British force attacked New Haven, Fairfield, and Norwalk. In Norwalk alone, 130 houses, 87 barns, 39 stores and shops, 4 mills, and 5 ships were burned. In September 1781, a raid on New London and Groton left both towns in ashes.

Many of the British raids were aimed at the home ports of America's vast privateer fleet. Privateers were commerce raiders: armed merchant ships authorized by Congress or state governments to capture British vessels. The privateers were almost all small ships: sloops, brigs, cutters, corvettes, and schooners. By one estimate, two thousand American ships sailed on privateering voyages during the Revolution. Their activities seriously inconvenienced the British army in America, while the military supplies from captured ships helped the Continental army through many a lean season. One of the most successful commerce raiders was the Continental schooner *Revenge*. Under the command of Captain Gustavus Conyngham, the *Revenge* captured an astonishing sixty vessels on an eighteen-month cruise in 1777–1778.

The Continental Navy

Congress authorized the formation of the Continental navy in October 1775. No one dreamed of building a fleet to match the mighty Royal Navy gun for gun. Rather, the American navy would depend on speed and surprise. Congress purchased some small, fast merchant ships and ordered the construction of thirteen large frigates—the cruisers of the day. The frigates would carry enough guns to fight the numerous British frigates in American waters and enough sail to outrun larger warships.

The navy's first major expedition met with success. Early in 1776, Commodore Esek Hopkins led an eight-ship task force to New Providence in the Bahamas. The Americans captured the port without opposition and carried off a large quantity of military supplies including eighty-eight cannon.

The navy was not to have much more good fortune. Several of its senior officers proved shockingly incompetent. The navy's administration was a disaster for years. Ship construction lagged.

Many of the best sailors preferred to sign aboard privateers for the higher pay and safer duty. The Continental frigates that did get to sea were soon captured or destroyed.

The Great Seaman

The navy's honor was saved by a handsome Scot of medium height, a stormy past, and a stupendous ambition: John Paul Jones. Born John Paul in 1747, he had gone to sea at the age of twelve. By his mid-twenties, he was a prosperous merchant captain in the West Indies. His future darkened, however, when he killed the leader of a mutiny. Fearing a lynching, he fled to America, where he adopted the last name Jones.

In 1775, he offered his services to the new Continental navy. He served with distinction aboard Hopkins's flagship *Alfred,* then proved himself a fearsome commerce raider as captain of the sloop *Providence* and later the *Alfred.*

The spring of 1778 found Jones steering his new ship, the sloop *Ranger,* from Brest, France, on one of the most daring raids of the war. He sailed up the west coast of England, picking off merchant ships with casual ease. Twice Jones landed men on the coast of Scotland to demand ransom in exchange for not destroying towns. The Royal Navy rushed ships to intercept Jones. On April 24, Jones pounded the British sloop *Drake* into surrender, then sailed calmly back to France.

The uproar in Britain was deafening. Newspapers screamed that the Royal Navy must capture "the pirate Paul Jones" at any cost. Safely in Brest, Jones turned over command of the *Ranger* to another captain on the promise he would soon receive a new French frigate. He waited six frustrating months while Benjamin Franklin tried to make good on the bargain. What Jones got instead was a large but aging merchantman, *Le Duc de Duras.* He renamed it the *Bonhomme Richard*—the "good man Richard"—in honor of Franklin, who had used the pen name Poor Richard in his famous almanac.

On August 14, 1779, Jones sailed the *Bonhomme Richard* out of Brest at the head of a seven-ship squadron, including two privateers. It was an uneasy little fleet. The second largest ship, the frigate *Alliance,* was commanded by a half-mad Frenchman, Pierre Landais, who hated Jones and took almost every opportunity to disobey orders. Other captains had doubts about Jones and his plans. The privateers soon thought better of sailing into British waters and slipped away. The smallest of Jones's warships became separated from the others and returned to France.

Despite the poor beginning, Jones kept to his plan. The squadron sailed around the west coast of Ireland, then north around Scotland, taking several merchant ships along the way. Sailing down the east coast of Scotland and England, the squadron terrorized coastal towns and shipping. On the afternoon of September 23, Jones ran across the prize he had been hoping for—a convoy of forty-one merchant ships escorted by two British warships, the fifty-gun frigate *Serapis* and the twenty-gun sloop *Countess of Scarborough.*

Battle by Moonlight

With four warships, Jones should have had the advantage, but the simmering insubordination in the squadron boiled up. The small corvette *Vengeance* sailed off to a safe distance. Landais ignored Jones's signals and steered the *Alliance* away from the coming fight. Only the frigate *Pallas* showed loyalty by engaging the *Scarborough.* That left the *Bonhomme Richard* to face the faster, better-armed *Serapis.*

The fight opened shortly after dark with an autumn moon rising over a mirror-smooth sea. The two ships sailed a pistol shot apart on a parallel course, their gunports open and the long rows of cannon thrust out. Sailors with burning matches stood ready. In an instant, either ship could fire a terrible "broadside" that would splinter wooden hulls and tear apart human bodies. Captain Richard Pearson of the *Serapis* demanded to know what ship he faced. Jones evaded the question for a moment as he maneuvered closer, then hoisted the American colors. Immediately, the two ships opened fire at a range of less than one hundred feet.

Two of *Richard*'s largest guns exploded the instant they were fired, killing the gunners and tearing a huge hole in the deck. The *Serapis*'s broadsides, heavier than *Richard*'s, crashed home with terrible effect. Within moments, Jones knew a gun duel with *Serapis* would be fatal. He must board the *Serapis* for a hand-to-hand fight.

Jones maneuvered to bring his ship against the stern of the *Serapis*, but Pearson saw through his plan and skillfully avoided it. In the course of the evasion, *Serapis* crossed in front of *Richard*. Looking down on *Richard*'s bloody decks, Pearson thought Jones might be ready to surrender. He called out, "Sir, has your ship struck [its flag]?"

Jones replied, "Sir, I have not yet begun to fight!"

Again the two ships swung onto a parallel course, cannons blazing. On the windward side, *Richard* was able to take advantage of a fresh gust of wind and surged ahead. Jones put his wheel over and tried to cross *Serapis*'s bow, a deadly maneuver that would allow *Richard*'s guns to sweep, or "rake," the exposed decks of Pearson's ship. He nearly made it across, then the bow of the *Serapis* rammed into *Richard*'s side. Rigging

John Paul Jones, commander of the
Bonhomme Richard, *directs his men in*
the attack on the frigate Serapis.

tangled and the ships swung together in a death embrace, bow to stern, their gun muzzles nearly touching.

The American and French marines aboard *Richard* swept the decks of *Serapis* with deadly fire, driving the British below, but *Serapis*'s guns continued to slam round after round into *Richard*'s shivering sides. Now Landais arrived on the scene. Instead of firing on *Serapis, Alliance* raked *Richard*'s decks, killing two sailors and wounding many others. Landais then sailed casually over to where *Pallas* had nearly defeated *Scarborough* but decided to help neither friend nor foe.

Richard's men fought on as water rose in their ship. For two furious hours, the battle raged. Fires burned on both ships. Boarding parties leaped across the narrow gap between the ships only to be thrown back in bloody fighting. On *Richard*'s quarterdeck, Jones himself served one of the nine-pound guns. At one point he slumped on a box in exhaustion. One of the sailors begged, "For God's sake, Captain, strike [the flag]!"

Jones leaped to his feet. "No, I will sink! I will never strike!" He returned to the cannon.

Alliance sailed by again and, despite the pleas of *Richard*'s crew, poured two more broadsides into the wounded ship. But *Serapis* and her brave captain were weakening too. A sailor from *Richard* crawled into the other ship's rigging and threw hand grenades into its hold. There was a tremendous roar as powder charges on the deck below exploded. Most of *Serapis*'s guns fell silent. As cannonballs from *Richard*'s quarterdeck guns threatened to dismast the British frigate, Pearson's nerve cracked. He struck his colors.

A strange silence fell over the bloody scene. Each ship had entered battle with about 325 men. Now more than half their crews lay dead or wounded. After a few stunned minutes, the men of both ships began putting out fires and caring for the wounded. Jones transferred to *Serapis* and, with *Richard* in tow, began limping toward friendly waters. *Richard* was beyond saving and sank on the morning of September 25. British warships swept the seas for Jones but failed to find his squadron before it slipped into a neutral Dutch harbor.

Alarm and Rejoicing

Jones's escape led to near panic in Britain's coastal towns. The Royal Navy was forced to increase patrols rather than sending much-needed ships to America. However, the bumbling American naval authorities never again gave Jones the means to bring the war to British home waters. They did, however, dismiss Pierre Landais from the navy—a mild punishment for his crimes.

Bonhomme Richard's victory over *Serapis* had little long-range importance, but it gave American morale a huge lift. The land war had taken a turn for the worse, with British forces threatening to overrun the South and the long-sought alliance between America and France turning sour. The dramatic story of the moonlit victory sent the patriots' spirits soaring.

★ 5 ★

Disaster in the South

In the autumn of 1778, the king's army sat once again in New York City, its long campaign in the Middle Atlantic colonies a dismal failure. The British had won most of the battles but had failed to crush the Revolution. More than three years of fighting in America had produced a deadlock. The British controlled the city, a few isolated forts, and Newport, Rhode Island, but nothing beyond. The Americans hung on to their dream of independence—too weak to win, too dedicated to give up.

The British government cast about for a new strategy to end the long, frustrating war. The solution seemed to lie in the South. Loyalist sympathy was strong in Georgia and the Carolinas. A British invasion might rally thousands to the king's banner. Meanwhile, the threat posed by British troops in New York City would prevent Washington from sending reinforcements to the small American army based in Charleston, South Carolina.

The plan seemed flawless. In a short time, the combined British and Loyalist forces would destroy rebel resistance in Georgia and the Carolinas. The British would then launch an

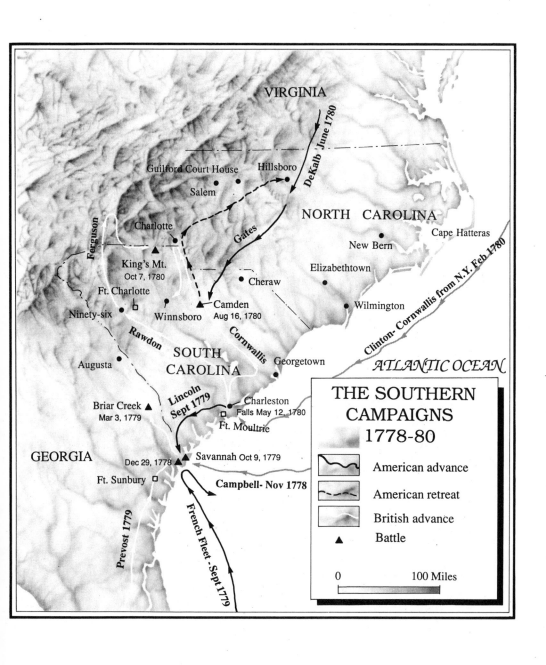

THE SOUTHERN
CAMPAIGNS
1778-80

American advance
American retreat
British advance
▲ Battle

0   100 Miles

invasion of Virginia from both north and south. The wealthiest colony would collapse and with it the Revolution.

The Invasion of Georgia

In late November 1778, General Clinton sent Lieutenant Colonel Archibald Campbell and an army of thirty-five hundred to invade Georgia. The British landed two days before Christmas, destroyed the small American force defending Savannah, and marched into the city on December 29. General Augustine Prevost arrived soon afterward with British reinforcements from Florida. By the end of January 1779, the British held a line of posts extending up the Savannah River to Augusta.

The great prize in the South was Charleston, the region's only major city and most important port. Charleston was defended by an American army of about three thousand under General Benjamin Lincoln, a solid but unimaginative officer. With part of the British army on garrison duty, Prevost could field about an equal number. The armies sparred like two boxers. Prevost tried to march north and suffered a minor defeat in early February. Lincoln tried to cross into Georgia and got thrashed at Briar Creek on March 3.

In late April, Lincoln tried again to recover Georgia, this time with an advance against Augusta. Prevost ignored Lincoln's move and made a dash for Charleston. General William Moultrie, the city's commander in Lincoln's absence, delayed Prevost's attack with skillful skirmishing and, as a last resort, a false offer to discuss surrender terms. Prevost caught on to the trick too late and was forced into defensive positions when Lincoln hurried back to the city. On June 20, Prevost's regulars splintered an attack led by Moultrie. A few days later, the British withdrew by sea.

Late in the summer of 1779, the Comte d'Estaing led the French fleet back into American waters to join Lincoln for a siege of Savannah. The allies opened the siege on October 4 with a tremendous bombardment of the outgunned and outmanned British garrison.

A typical eighteenth-century siege involved a great deal of digging. The commander of the attacking force would choose what he considered a weak point in the enemy fortifications and order a long trench dug to run parallel to the enemy lines. From this first parallel, soldiers would push trenches called approaches in zigzag lines toward the enemy fortifications. At a point several hundred yards closer, they would start digging a second parallel. Eventually, the attackers might dig three, four, or even more parallels.

The defenders would do their best to strengthen fortifications and disrupt the digging with raids called sorties. However, the advantage usually lay with the attackers. As the digging advanced, they would bring cannon forward to fire on the city with greater effect. From a parallel close to the city, they could dig tunnels called saps under the fortifications. A sap packed with a huge charge of gunpowder could blow a gaping hole in the strongest defenses.

The final step in a siege required infantry to make a frontal assault on the fortifications through the holes blasted by cannon and saps. Many sieges ended well before this final stage when defenders broke under the combined weight of bombardment, fatigue, and short rations.

A strongly defended city might hold out for weeks or even months, but Lincoln expected Savannah to surrender in a few days. His estimate was probably correct, but d'Estaing grew im-

A British redoubt holds out against a French and American assault during the siege of Savannah.

patient. He worried that the British fleet might catch his ships at anchor. He demanded an end to the deliberate siege tactics. Lincoln reluctantly agreed to an early assault.

The allies attacked shortly before dawn on October 9. Alerted by a deserter, the British were waiting for them. The result was a tremendous slaughter. Grapeshot and massed musket fire from the fortifications tore huge holes in the allied ranks. Stumbling over the bodies of the fallen, the French and Americans pressed forward. They reached the ditch surrounding the fortifications, but the wall on the far side was too high to climb. They swirled in a desperate mass trying to find a way through. Then a regiment of British grenadiers appeared from nowhere and smashed into their midst. In a savage hand-to-hand fight, the grenadiers drove the allies back.

Not since the battle of Bunker Hill in 1775 had the Revolution seen such terrible close-quarter fighting. The French and Americans lost 828 men—dead and wounded—nearly one-fifth of the attacking force. Among the dead was Count Casimir Pulaski, a gallant Polish volunteer in the American cause. The British losses amounted to 155. Georgia was lost. D'Estaing sailed for the West Indies, and Lincoln led his battered army back to Charleston.

Charleston

It would soon be the Americans' turn to suffer a siege. On December 26, 1779—almost a year to the day after the British capture of Savannah—fourteen British warships and some ninety transports sailed south from New York City. Aboard were eighty-five hundred men under General Clinton and his second-in-command, Lord Charles Cornwallis. After a stormy passage, the army landed on February 11, 1780, at Johns Island, thirty miles south of Charleston.

General Lincoln strengthened Charleston's defenses and pulled all available troops into the city. With nearly six thousand continentals, militia, and armed citizens, he felt confident that he could hold the city.

Clinton prepared for the march on Charleston with grim thoroughness. He had a grudge to settle. In June 1776, he had failed to take the city by sea when Royal Navy frigates had suffered a terrific beating in a day-long shoot-out with the American defenders of Sullivan's Island at the harbor entrance. Clinton was determined to avenge the greatest setback of his career.

Six weeks after landing, Clinton occupied the landward approaches above Charleston. The city stood at the foot of a peninsula where the Ashley and Cooper rivers joined to flow into the sea. Clinton's troops started placing batteries and digging parallels eight hundred yards from the American lines. Eight Royal Navy frigates successfully ran the harbor defenses to cut off an evacuation by sea.

On April 13, the city's agony began. British cannon began firing red-hot shot and shells filled with inflammable material into the city. As the city's inhabitants fought the spreading fires, the British guns fired exploding shells that cut down men, women, and children with bursts of jagged metal. After two hours, the British guns fell silent. Slowly, the citizens brought the fires under control.

At any time in the next few weeks, Clinton could have burned Charleston to the ground with a longer bombardment. However, he was a humane man and not anxious to inflict pointless suffering on the people of Charleston. Furthermore, he knew that destroying the city would enrage the South and damage his efforts to recruit supporters for the king.

The fighting increased as the British trenches crept closer to the American lines. The two sides blazed away at each other with cannon and muskets. Short of grapeshot, the Americans fired glass, pottery, and every kind of metal scrap they could find—broken shovels, hatchets, pickaxes, flatirons, and the metal from spent British shells. The Americans launched night sorties that further increased the casualties. Clinton grimly kept his men digging. Lincoln secretly offered to surrender the city if he could march his troops away. Clinton laughed at the absurd trade.

By early May, the British parallels were within yards of the American lines. On the night of May 9, two hundred American guns opened a fearsome but pointless barrage. Clinton lost patience. He unleashed the full power of his batteries. Soon the city was ablaze with dozens of fires. The courage of the townspeople broke, and the civilian authorities gave Lincoln permission to surrender. After two days of negotiations, Lincoln turned over the South's most important city, its garrison of 5,466 men, and a tremendous amount of equipment, including 391 cannon and 5,916 muskets.

Dark Months

The defeat at Charleston sent the American cause reeling. In the populous North, the loss of a single major city made little difference. Trade could be rerouted as farmers and merchants adjusted to the new conditions. Not so in the sparsely settled South, where Charleston was the *only* major city.

Even more serious was the threat of civil war in the South. The Loyalists—or Tories, as they were often called—had been waiting a long time to strike at the patriots. At the war's outbreak, they had rallied to the king in large numbers. However, patriot forces had driven most of the Loyalists into hiding with a crushing victory at Moore's Creek Bridge near Cross Creek (today's Fayetteville), North Carolina, on February 27, 1776.

The British invasion of Georgia and South Carolina gave the Loyalists a chance to settle scores. Mounted raiders swept down on farms and villages to loot, burn, and murder. Units of Tory and patriot irregulars clashed in small, savage battles. The winners—Tory or patriot—often bayonetted the wounded and hung the prisoners.

From Georgetown to Ninety-Six

Clinton moved quickly to extend British control across South Carolina. He established a strong post at Camden and lesser posts at Georgetown and Ninety-Six. To man his strongpoints, he used regular units or Loyalist units from the North. Meanwhile, local Tory militia occupied many villages, ferries, and crossroads.

Between the posts, Lieutenant Colonel Banastre Tarleton roved with his feared British Legion of Tory cavalry. Tarleton was twenty-six, a short, muscular, handsome man from an English merchant family. He was daring, energetic, and resourceful, but also ruthless and cruel. No other British officer became so widely hated by the Americans.

After the fall of Charleston, Tarleton pursued about 400 Virginia continentals who had arrived too late to reinforce the city. Tarleton's men rode 154 miles in fifty-four hours, catching the continentals near the North Carolina border. A cavalry charge broke the American ranks. The survivors huddled together, raised a white flag, and called out for "quarter," a common term for mercy to the defeated. The Tories answered with swords and bayonets. The massacre left 113 continentals dead and 150 too badly wounded to be moved. The Tories marched about 50 prisoners away, while perhaps 100 continentals escaped to tell of the slaughter. Before long a bitter new phrase, "Tarleton's quarter," was added to the American vocabulary. Henceforth, the Americans could expect no quarter—nor would they readily give it. War in the North had usually been fought according to almost polite standards of conduct. But in the civil war in the South, there would be few rules and little mercy.

The Bad News Spreads

At Morristown in New Jersey, George Washington listened to reports from the South in deep frustration. He could not abandon his northern base. The majority of the British army still lay in New York City. Any day the British might resume the war in the Middle Atlantic colonies. Washington must be there to oppose them.

His army had survived another brutally hard winter—but only barely. Unpaid, hungry, and cold, the men had grown mutinous. Only Washington's presence had prevented a complete collapse of the army. Washington wrote strong letters to Congress, demanding food, clothing, and money. But Congress had little real power and could only beg the states to send more aid. Little arrived for the army. Not since the grim winter of 1776–1777 had civilian morale fallen so low. The American economy staggered. A Continental dollar was hardly worth the price of its flimsy paper. A good pair of boots might cost $600, a horse $20,000!

Washington had to find some way to revive hope in the American cause. He could not spare men for a campaign in the South, but he had to send them anyway. He selected the best: fourteen hundred Maryland and Delaware continentals under the command of Major General Baron De Kalb. De Kalb, a towering German, had arrived with Lafayette. A veteran of the Seven Years' War, he was no more a baron than his countryman Steuben. However, he was an extraordinary soldier—unfailingly brave, skillful, and honest. For the "exercise," he would march with his men rather than ride a horse. And if he decided to march into Hell, the continentals would follow him.

The Brutal March South

The continentals trudged south in the blazing heat of the early summer of 1780. They had few wagons, and the men carried most of the supplies on their aching backs. They were tormented by insects and thirst. They had expected to live off the land, but the pickings were slim, and the men often marched for days on empty bellies. Yet, they kept marching. On June 22, De Kalb led his men into Hillsboro, North Carolina.

He let them rest for a week while he contacted the small bands of daring fighters—called guerrillas by later generations—who were struggling to keep the patriot cause alive in South Carolina. The guerrilla chieftains Thomas Sumter, Andrew Pickens, and Francis Marion—the famed "Swamp Fox"— sent reports that a major victory by De Kalb would rally thousands of patriots. Delay or defeat would swing public opinion to the Tories. De Kalb formed a plan to attack the British at Camden, then sent out detachments to recruit every available militia unit.

Gates Takes Command

The undeserved reputation of General Horatio Gates thwarted De Kalb's plans. Congress loved Gates, the skilled political gen-

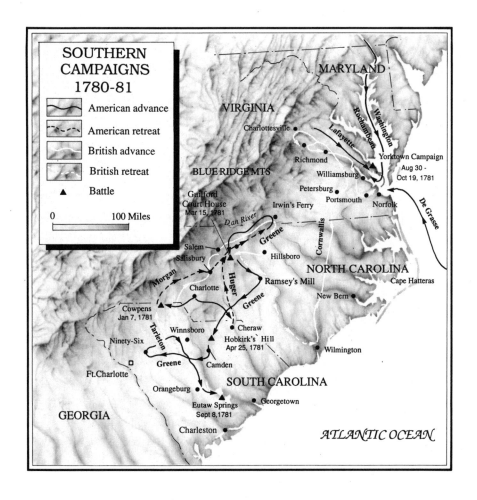

SOUTHERN CAMPAIGNS 1780-81

- American advance
- American retreat
- British advance
- British retreat
- ▲ Battle

0   100 Miles

MARYLAND

VIRGINIA

Charlottesville

Rochambeau

Washington

Lafayette

Richmond

Yorktown Campaign
Aug 30 -
Oct 19, 1781

BLUE RIDGE MTS

Williamsburg

Petersburg

Portsmouth

Norfolk

De Grasse

Guilford
Court House
Mar 15, 1781

Irwin's Ferry

Dan River

Greene

Cornwallis

Salem

Salisbury

Hillsboro

NORTH CAROLINA

Cape Hatteras

Morgan

Charlotte

Huger

Ramsey's Mill

Greene

New Bern

Cowpens
Jan 7, 1781

Tarleton

Greene

Winnsboro

Cheraw

Ninety-Six

Hobkirk's Hill
Apr 25, 1781

Wilmington

Greene

Camden

Ft.Charlotte

Orangeburg

SOUTH CAROLINA

GEORGIA

Eutaw Springs
Sept 8,1781

Georgetown

Charleston

ATLANTIC OCEAN

eral who had accepted Burgoyne's surrender at Saratoga. Few outside the army knew that Benedict Arnold had really won the great victory in northern New York. Without Washington's approval, Congress dispatched Gates to take command of the southern army.

On July 25, Gates arrived at De Kalb's camp south of Hillsboro. De Kalb accepted his demotion politely and explained the route he had chosen for the march on Camden. Gates would have none of it. He chose a shorter but more difficult road through Tory country. De Kalb and his officers tried to point out that the army would find little food and no recruits along the way. Gates would not be swayed. On July 27, the army marched toward Camden.

The suffering of the men in the next two weeks made the earlier march seem like a garden stroll. One veteran reported that each man received only half a pound of flour and half a pound of nearly inedible beef in the entire time. When mutiny threatened, De Kalb and his officers quieted the men with praise for their endurance.

Camden

The army staggered into the vicinity of Camden on August 14. Cornwallis had heard of the American approach in time to rush to the scene with reinforcements. At forty-two, Cornwallis was a formidable general, perhaps the best field tactician in the British army. He had suffered as the cautious Clinton's deputy. But Clinton had returned to New York, and Cornwallis at last had his chance for glory. He had only about twenty-two hundred men at Camden, but they were almost all seasoned regulars as eager for battle as their commander.

Gates had the absurd idea that the addition of militia units had increased his army to seven thousand men. His senior aide, or adjutant, Colonel Otho Williams, checked and reported to Gates that only slightly over three thousand—mostly raw militia—were present and fit for duty. Perhaps a few hundred more would be ready to march by morning, but— Angrily, Gates cut off Williams's report. "Sir, there are more than enough for our purpose!" To Williams's horror, Gates then ordered a long night march on Camden.

The exhausted troops stumbled along in the dark. About 10:00 P.M., they collided with a British column. By chance, Cornwallis had ordered a night march along the same road. Tarleton's cavalry charged and broke the head of the American column. The continentals at the center drove the horsemen off. Both armies pulled back to wait for daylight.

The battleground that chance had chosen was a thin forest of pine flanked by wide swamps. Gates placed his militia on the left and most of his continentals on the right. Safely behind the lines, he waited with a reserve of Maryland continentals. Cornwallis stretched his force in a line six hundred yards away, holding two regiments of Scottish regulars and Tarleton's cavalry in reserve.

The British right moved forward at first light. Gates ordered the Virginia militia on his far left to meet them. It was the last order he would issue that day. The redcoats fired, then charged with the bayonet. The Virginians had never seen a battle before. They stared at the onrushing rows of steel, threw down their muskets, and ran. Immediately, the nearly two thousand North Carolina militia in the center turned tail.

The continentals on the right stood alone to meet the charge of the entire British line. Desperately, Williams tried to bring the Maryland reserve forward, but it was pushed back by the charging British. Nearly surrounded, De Kalb and the remaining six hundred continentals fought like demons. They withstood charge after charge, then hurled themselves against the British line, broke through, and wheeled to hit the British rear. For a few wild minutes, De Kalb and his men actually believed

*Baron de Kalb is mortally wounded
at the Battle of Camden.*

they were winning. Then Tarleton's cavalry thundered down on them. The shock tore the American regiments apart. The British infantry finished the job with the bayonet.

De Kalb lay bleeding to death from eleven wounds. British soldiers propped him against a wagon and began stripping his body for souvenirs. Cornwallis angrily interrupted the scene and ordered De Kalb's wounds treated. The powerful German died three days later. By then Gates had arrived in Hillsboro, 180 miles from the battlefield. He had not waited to see the continentals' valiant stand but had mounted the fastest horse in the army and soon outdistanced the fleeing militia.

One historian has called the battle of Camden "the most disastrous defeat ever inflicted on an American army." About 650 continentals and 400 militiamen had been killed or captured. Most of the militiamen who escaped decided to go home rather than face another battle. Only about 700 exhausted survivors straggled into Hillsboro. They were all that remained of Gates's army.

★ 6 ★

———The Amazing Campaign———

Camden virtually destroyed the American army in the South. The British southern strategy seemed about to win the war. Yet, Lord Cornwallis felt uneasy as he prepared for the march into North Carolina. The southern Tories had not joined the British in their expected thousands. He could not even count on them to provide food for his army or news of rebel movements. Meanwhile, guerrillas continued to plague him, sniping at his sentries and ambushing his scouts and foraging parties. How many battles must the army win before the rebels finally gave up their "glorious cause"?

King's Mountain

While Cornwallis tried to quiet his unease, a strange, savage confrontation was building in the rough country north of Ninety-Six. Since the fall of Charleston, a strong Tory force had been policing the country between the Saluda and Catawba rivers. In command was a brave and highly capable British officer, Patrick Ferguson. In over twenty years of service, Ferguson had been overlooked by his superiors. Only a major at the age of thirty-six, Ferguson viewed his assignment as a great opportunity to prove himself.

Ferguson's troops burned and looted mercilessly, earning the deep hatred of the area's patriots. In late September 1780, patriot militiamen from the Carolinas and Virginia gathered to strike back. They were joined by a large band of "over-mountain" men from what is today Tennessee. These rugged frontiersmen were equipped with deadly-accurate Deckhard rifles and all the skills of wilderness fighting.

On hearing of the forces mustering to fight him, Ferguson retreated to King's Mountain on the North Carolina border. The mountain was actually a narrow plateau some 60 feet high and 500 yards long. Ferguson established a strong position and defied "God Almighty and all the rebels out of Hell to overcome him."

Ferguson had about one thousand men in camp at noon on October 7 when a force of nine hundred patriots surrounded King's Mountain. The patriots stormed the steep slopes, yelling Indian war cries. Ferguson drove them off with bayonet charges, but the patriots took cover behind trees and picked off the Tories at will.

Casualties mounted as the noose tightened. Ferguson refused to surrender, cutting down two white flags with his sword. The terrified Tories crowded together behind wagons at the northeast end of the plateau. Ferguson tried to rally them. He mounted his beautiful white horse to lead a charge. A patriot rifleman drew aim and shot him from the saddle.

Their leader dead, the Tories tried to surrender. The pa-

*At the Battle of King's Mountain, patriot militia-
men from the Carolinas and Virginia, joined
by a large band of backwoodsmen, take their
revenge on the Tories. In the background of this
print, the British officer Patrick Ferguson has
just been shot from his beautiful white horse.*

triots shouted "Tarleton's quarter" and kept shooting. They had no single commander, and it took a long time for their officers to finally end the slaughter. The battle had cost the patriots 28 killed and 62 wounded. Of Ferguson's force, 157 lay dead and 163 were too badly wounded to be moved. The remaining 698 were marched away as prisoners. Nine of them were later hung, and many others suffered harsh treatment at the hands of bitter patriots. Patrick Ferguson had been the only non-American in the brutal fight.

News of the disaster reached Cornwallis at Charlotte, North Carolina, where he had paused to rest his army on the march to Virginia. Hysterical reports greatly magnified the size of the actual rebel force. Cornwallis turned around and made for Winnsboro, midway between his endangered posts at Camden and Ninety-Six. It rained steadily. The men marched muddy, cold, and hungry. American militia hung on the column's flanks, picking off any soldier who wandered. The British arrived at Winnsboro at the end of October but found no large rebel force to oppose them. Most of the victors of King's Mountain had gone home.

Greene Takes Command

General Gates brought the remains of his "grand army of the southern department" from Hillsboro to Charlotte in the wake of Cornwallis's departure from North Carolina. On December 2, 1780, Major General Nathanael Greene arrived to take command. The two generals exchanged polite greetings, then Gates rode off into a long overdue disgrace.

Greene surveyed his army of fifteen hundred men. They were a sorry-looking lot. Few had decent clothing or adequate weapons. Greene summoned his supply officer and learned that the army had only three days' rations. All night, Greene asked his staff questions. One officer later wrote that "by the following morning he understood [the situation] better than Gates had done in the whole period of his command."

What amazed the staff officer would not have surprised Washington. Since early in the war, Greene had been Washington's strong right arm. The tall, handsome Rhode Islander had distinguished himself in a dozen battles. When Washington had needed a quartermaster general to straighten out the army's supply system, he had turned to Greene. Protesting that history never remembered quartermasters, Greene nevertheless threw himself into the job, somehow finding the supplies to keep Washington's army going. When Congress had asked Washington to appoint a new commander of the southern army, the choice had been easy.

At thirty-eight, Greene had experience, a fine mind, and a knack for spotting talent. His army might be small, but it had a core of tough continentals and an exceptional number of excellent officers. First among the officers was the "Old Wagoner," Brigadier General Daniel Morgan. A big bear of a man, Morgan was perhaps the best leader of militia troops in the army. In 1775, he and his Virginia riflemen had survived the terrible march into Canada on Benedict Arnold's ill-fated attempt to take Quebec. In 1777, Morgan had played a major role in winning the battles that led to the British surrender at Saratoga. But Congress had given all the honors to its darling Gates. Disgusted and in poor health, Morgan had retired to his Virginia home. News of the disaster at Camden brought him back to the fight. Greene could not have asked for a better second-in-command.

A *Daring Strategy*

Greene quickly concluded that he could not defeat Cornwallis in battle until the American army gained strength. However, he could drive Cornwallis crazy in the meantime. He chose a daring strategy that defied all the wisdom of the military textbooks. In the face of a superior force, he would divide his army. Morgan would take some six hundred of the best men west toward King's Mountain. Greene would take the rest of the army east to Cheraw where it could rest, recruit, and refit. If Cornwallis marched from Winnsboro on Cheraw, Morgan would strike at Ninety-Six. If Cornwallis moved on Morgan, Greene would advance on Charleston. And, if Cornwallis responded to the American moves by dividing his own army, perhaps Greene or Morgan could win a round.

Morgan set out with orders to act "offensively or defensively as your prudence and discretion may direct." These excellent orders displayed Greene at his best—he trusted his subordinate's judgment. If Morgan won glory on his own, Greene would give him full credit.

Greene turned to coordinating efforts with the guerrilla commanders. Long ignored by Gates, Sumter, Pickens, and Marion responded to Greene's cordial messages by increasing their raids. Greene sent Lieutenant Colonel Henry Lee and three hundred elite cavalrymen to cooperate with Marion along the Pee Dee River north of Georgetown. In "Light-Horse Harry" Lee, the Americans had a match for Tarleton. (Lee's son, Robert E. Lee, would win undying fame as the Confederate commander in the Civil War.)

Meanwhile, Lieutenant Colonel William Washington, a cousin of the commander in chief, led Morgan's cavalry on a rampage across the west. Near Ninety-Six, the American cavalry destroyed a force of 250 Tories, killing, wounding, or capturing all but a handful.

Cornwallis Acts

Cornwallis was dumbfounded by Greene's moves. Was Greene a fool or the most dangerous of opponents: a general who wrote his own rules? Cornwallis studied the maps and decided to divide his army of four thousand into three parts. General Alexander Leslie would take one part to Camden to block any move Greene made from Cheraw. A fast-moving force under Tarleton would go after Morgan. Cornwallis would lead the main army into North Carolina to cut off Morgan's retreat.

Cornwallis could find no fault with his plan. Each of his three forces would match in size and certainly outmatch in quality any force Greene could field. Charleston and the other major British posts had strong garrisons that could withstand any attack until relief arrived. Now for Morgan. Tarleton would be the hammer, Cornwallis the anvil, and Morgan the eggshell between.

Cowpens

Banastre Tarleton, the most feared cavalry commander in the British army, set out after Morgan with a mixed force of eleven hundred infantry and horsemen. With new recruits, Morgan had a nearly equal number of men, but only a third were continentals and the rest unreliable militia. Nevertheless, Morgan was delighted to hear news of Tarleton's pursuit. Most American officers considered militia nearly worthless in battle, but Morgan knew how to make them fight.

Morgan chose to make his stand at Cowpens, a thinly wooded plain used by local farmers as a roundup spot for roaming cattle. Some of his officers objected that Cowpens was a natural trap. Without swamps or thick woods on either side, the army's flanks would "hang in the air," vulnerable to encirclement by Tarleton's vastly superior force of cavalry. Behind the American lines, the Broad River cut off retreat. Morgan knew what he was doing. Without a handy hiding place or an open line of retreat, the militia would stand and fight.

On the night of January 16, 1781, the "Old Wagoner" toured his camp. He sat down with the men, sharing a drink of rum and joking about the surprise he had waiting for "Banny" Tarleton. Over and over, he told the militiamen, "Just hold up your heads, boys. Give them two fires and you're free."

At dawn, Morgan formed his main line of about 450 men on a low ridge. The continentals would hold the center and the best of the militia—many of them veterans of the Continental army—the wings. About 150 yards in front of the main line, Morgan posted 300 militia under the guerrilla chief Andrew Pickens. Another 150 yards in front of that line, 150 picked riflemen formed a thin skirmishing line intended to slow the British advance. To the rear of the main line, 125 cavalrymen under Colonel Washington lay hidden by a low hill. Every man in the army took his place knowing Morgan's plan—there would be no generals' secrets on this day when free men stood against the forces of tyranny.

Tarleton Attacks

Tarleton's army came to Cowpens about 8:00 A.M. after a hard night march. Immediately, Tarleton hurled his cavalry against the American line of skirmishers. The riflemen took cover and

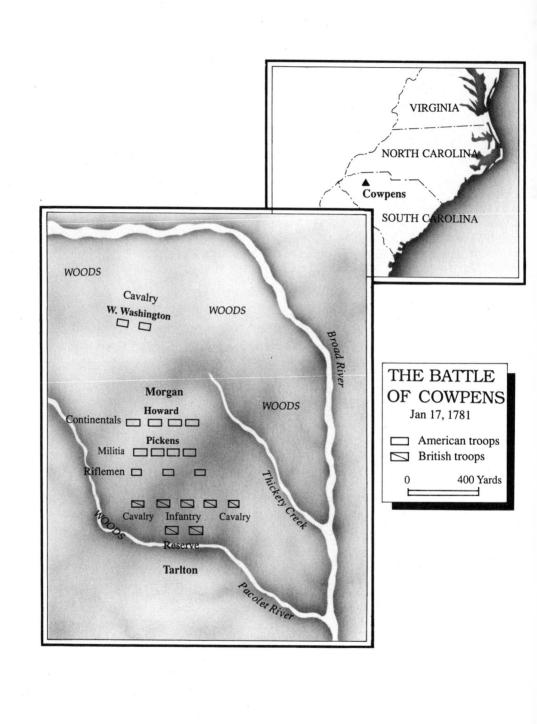

VIRGINIA

NORTH CAROLINA

▲ Cowpens

SOUTH CAROLINA

WOODS

Cavalry
W. Washington

WOODS

Broad River

Morgan

WOODS

Howard
Continentals

Pickens
Militia

Riflemen

Thickety Creek

Cavalry   Infantry   Cavalry

Reserve

WOODS

Tarlton

Pacolet River

THE BATTLE
OF COWPENS
Jan 17, 1781

☐ American troops
▨ British troops

0   400 Yards

drove them back with heavy losses. Then, firing at will, they withdrew to join Pickens and his men in the second line. In most battles, the sight of the smallest retreat threw militia into panic. But this time everyone knew that the withdrawal was part of Morgan's plan.

Tarleton formed his men for battle, placing his light infantry on the right, his Tory Legion infantry in the center, and his regular British infantry on the left. On either flank, he posted cavalry. His remaining cavalry and the feared Scottish Highland regulars stayed in reserve behind the line.

The British line advanced to the steady drumbeat that had marked approaching doom in so many earlier battles. The militiamen waited, remembering Morgan's promise, "two fires and you're free." When the British reached killing range, Pickens gave the order. The militia fired a deadly volley, reloaded, and fired again. The shock staggered the British line. It wavered, then came on again. Through the billows of powder smoke, the British could see the militia running toward the American left. Tarleton's cavalry swept down on the retreating militia. Colonel Washington's cavalrymen sprang from their hiding place behind the American lines. For the second time that day, Tarleton's proud horsemen fled in disorder.

Morgan's plan was working to perfection. Tarleton's infantry came on, convinced that another victory was only moments away. They charged up the ridge toward the main American line, commanded by Lieutenant Colonel John Howard. The continentals knelt to steady their weapons and delivered a withering fire. The British attack stumbled to a halt. For half an hour the two lines blazed away at each other.

Tarleton ordered his Highlanders forward to outflank the American right. Howard saw the move coming. He ordered the company on his far right to swing back at right angles to the line. Suddenly, Morgan's plan came apart. Howard's order was misunderstood. Instead of preparing to meet the Highlanders' charge, the Americans on the far right faced about and marched over the ridge to the rear! Thinking a retreat had been ordered, officers on the center and left ordered their men to follow.

Tarleton saw the retreat and believed victory was in his grasp. He ordered an all-out pursuit. His men cheered, broke ranks, and charged up the ridge. They did not see the Americans halt on the small hill behind and face about as Morgan and Howard regained control. At the critical moment, Pickens led the militia back onto the field to form on Howard's right.

The British crested the ridge in a mob and came howling down the far side straight into the muzzles of nearly a thousand American muskets. The tremendous blast shattered the British regiments. "Give them the bayonet," Howard yelled. The continentals hurled themselves into the mass of bleeding, deafened men. Washington's cavalry smashed into the British rear. In a few minutes, the fight was over; the British threw down their arms and begged for quarter.

Morgan had won the most complete American victory of the war. Tarleton escaped with a few cavalry, but he left behind 100 men dead, 229 wounded, and 600 prisoners—90 percent of his force. Twelve Americans had been killed and 60 wounded.

Escape to the North

Morgan was far too wise to waste time enjoying his victory. He had broken the hammer, but Cornwallis was nearby and could drop the anvil on him yet. Two hours after the British surrender, Morgan had his army marching north to escape Cornwallis's trap. His objective was the crossroads at Ramsour's Mill, North Carolina, a hundred mountainous miles to the northeast.

Beyond the crossroads he might find Greene and the rest of the American army.

Cornwallis received news of Tarleton's disaster that evening. He was a scant twenty-five miles from Cowpens and perfectly positioned to head off Morgan at Ramsour's Mill. Through the next day, he waited anxiously for the arrival of a supply column. On January 19, he set out to close the trap on Morgan. His well-fed, disciplined troops marched fast, but the Americans marched faster. The British arrived at Ramsour's Mill on January 25, only to learn that the Americans had marched through two days before.

Cornwallis was determined to run Morgan to earth. At Ramsour's Mill, he ordered all but essential supplies destroyed. He set the example by burning his own books and spare uniforms. The enlisted men watched sadly as the army's rum casks were broken open and their precious contents spilled. Two days later, a lean and thoroughly mean army got back on the road.

The Race to the Dan

On the far side of the Catawba River, Morgan rested his army. Escorted by a handful of cavalry, Greene rode the 125 miles through Tory country from Cheraw to Morgan's camp, arriving on January 30. The two generals discussed a plan. They were still too weak to fight Cornwallis, but perhaps they could march him into the ground. They would head for Salisbury, where General Isaac Huger would join them with the troops from Cheraw. Then they would make a dash northeast to the Dan River on the southern border of Virginia. Beyond the wide, deep Dan, they would enjoy supplies and safety. Stranded on the North Carolina shore, Cornwallis would find himself far from his supply depots and deep in hostile country.

The famous, deadly Race to the Dan was on. The two armies marched in nearly indescribable misery. A steady, cold rain fell day after day, swelling the icy creeks and turning the roads to deep mud. The Americans marched sick, hungry, and cold. Wet boots came apart, leaving many soldiers barefoot. Yet, they kept marching, often making more than twenty miles a day—an extraordinary pace under the terrible conditions. Behind them, the British came on, doggedly trying to make up the miles separating the armies.

Delayed by flooded creeks and swamps, Huger could not make it to Salisbury in time. Greene redirected him northeast toward Guilford Court House. He and Morgan led their troops due north to decoy Cornwallis away from Guilford, then turned east and marched rapidly to join Huger on February 6.

By unspoken agreement, Greene and Cornwallis called a halt to the killing pace. The Americans rested four days at Guilford. Twenty-five miles away, the British camped at Salem. Greene liked the lay of the land around Guilford and briefly considered making a stand. His better judgment argued against it. Cornwallis outnumbered him three thousand to two thousand. Morgan was so ill with fever and rheumatism that Greene had to order him home. It was not yet time to fight. He would make for Irwin's Ferry, seventy miles away on the Dan.

Greene's army began the final sprint for the Dan on February 10, while Colonel Otho Williams with seven hundred picked infantry and Lee's cavalry maneuvered to decoy Cornwallis away from the ferry. For four days, Cornwallis chased Williams relentlessly. Again and again, Lee's Legion fought off the British cavalry. Often the head of the British column and the American rear guard were within pistol shot. Surviving on three hours of sleep a night and one meal a day, the Americans kept ahead.

Williams received messages from Greene. On February 13, Greene wrote that he had sent the baggage train ahead to the ferry. A few hours later, another message told Williams that Greene had arrived at the Dan. Finally, at noon on the 14th, Williams read, "All our troops are over and the stage is clear." He spread the word. His exhausted men cheered and pushed on with new energy. Fourteen miles lay between them and the ferry.

At sunset, Williams's infantry reached the Dan after covering forty miles in sixteen hours. They clambered into the boats and pulled for the far shore. Lee's cavalry dashed onto the riverbank, dismounted, and leaped into the last few boats. The sight of the swift water frightened the horses, but they responded to the pull on their bridles and swam across. The last of Greene's army reached the Virginia shore just as the British cavalry galloped to the riverbank. Not a single boat remained to carry the British across. The Americans had won the race.

Cornwallis Retreats

Cornwallis's army stumbled south. Some 230 miles lay between it and the nearest British supply depot, an impossible distance for the exhausted army. Cornwallis camped at the abandoned American depot at Hillsboro. He hoped to get supplies and reinforcements from local Tories. Greene was not about to let that happen. A few days after the escape, Lee, Pickens, and Williams recrossed the Dan with orders to throttle Tory activity.

Lee and Pickens caught up with a party of four hundred mounted Tories hurrying to join Cornwallis. Lee's men wore green uniforms similar to those of Tarleton's cavalry. Lee sent a request to the Tory commander asking him to draw his troops to the side of the road so "Colonel Tarleton's men might pass with ease." The Tory commander complied. Lee's men rode even with the Tories, wheeled, and attacked. Ninety Tories died and most of the rest were wounded, all without cost to the Americans. The incident discouraged any more Tories from joining Cornwallis. The Americans patrolled the countryside, chopping up British foraging parties and keeping a watch on Cornwallis's activities.

Guilford Court House

Reinforced by a strong detachment of Virginia riflemen, Greene brought the rest of the army back into North Carolina on February 23. For two weeks, he maneuvered as more militia joined the army. By the second week in March, he had an army of forty-four hundred men. At last, Greene was strong enough for battle. He marched to Guilford Court House, where he had thought of fighting five weeks before.

Cornwallis was camped twelve miles from Guilford when his scouts brought word of Greene's latest move. With only nineteen hundred men fit for duty, Cornwallis had a ready excuse for retreat. Instead, he accepted the American challenge—the honor of the British army was at stake.

The British arrived on the battlefield at noon on March 15 to find the American troops already in battle formation. Greene had placed one thousand North Carolina militia on either side of a road running through a broad clearing. Hidden in the woods to left and right were detachments of more than three hundred veteran infantry and cavalry. Three hundred yards behind the first line, stood a line of twelve hundred reliable Virginia militia. Another 550 yards behind the second, the main American line of fourteen hundred continentals occupied a ridge on the left side of the road.

The British attacked about 1:30 P.M. on a clear, cold afternoon. The North Carolina militia steadied their muskets on a fence and delivered two withering volleys. Then, following Greene's instructions, they turned and ran to the rear to reform. The veterans in the woods waited until the advancing British line came abreast, then fired yet another terrible volley. Never before had the iron discipline of the British infantry been more in evidence. The flank companies split off to engage the Americans in the woods. The main line, reinforced by the reserves, marched on against the second American line. Again the compact British ranks took terrible losses under the deliberate American fire.

Under a furious assault, the Virginia militia gave ground slowly until they were pushed through the woods to the right of the road. As they withdrew, the British line pivoted to the left to attack the main American line. The British casualties had already reached high numbers, but on they came. A raw Continental regiment broke and ran, but Greene plugged the hole in the line. The main line loosed a deadly volley. The British line staggered, got its balance, and charged. The Americans threw them back. The British charged again. The fight became hand-to-hand, and the Americans' superiority in numbers began to tell. The British could not advance or retreat, but only hold position and slug it out.

Cornwallis watched his army about to be overwhelmed. He made a fearful decision—he ordered his gunners to fire grapeshot into the tangled mass of fighting men. An officer begged him not to do it. Cornwallis turned away and the guns roared. The grapeshot tore into British and American soldiers alike. Those who survived retreated.

As the Americans recovered, Greene considered attacking, but there was risk. His ranks were disordered, his men exhausted. British discipline could yet win the day. He ordered a retreat. Cornwallis was left holding the field. His officers called it a victory; their general knew better.

American Victory

Cornwallis could count. The battle of Guilford Court House had cost him 532 dead and wounded, against 260 American casualties. He had started the campaign in January with more than 4,000 men. Fewer than 1,400 remained fit for duty. Greene had marched and bled the British army nearly to death. Two days later, the best field general in the British army admitted defeat and began his withdrawal from the South.

★ 7 ★

The Tide Turns

After Guilford Court House, the tide of war turned in the Revolution's favor. Cornwallis marched north, hoping to somehow win the war with victories in Virginia. Greene dispatched his lieutenants to pick off the British and Tory outposts in the Carolinas and Georgia. By the early summer of 1781, no inland post remained in British hands. The Tories drifted back to their villages and farms; the civil war in the South was over.

Twice the Americans fought battles with the small British army that remained in South Carolina. At Hobkirk's Hill in April and Eutaw Springs in September, the British were left holding battlegrounds littered with redcoat dead. Like Cornwallis at Guilford, the British commanders could claim victory, but the casualty lists told a different story. Unable to afford any more bloody victories, the British withdrew to Charleston.

The Lion at Bay

Cornwallis raided along the James River in the summer of 1781, but could not lure the small American army in Virginia into

*General Cornwallis offers his sword to
George Washington as he surrenders at
Yorktown, Virginia, October 19, 1781.
The war was over at last.*

battle. Generals Steuben and Lafayette maneuvered at a safe distance, biding their time. Finally, Cornwallis withdrew to Yorktown on the coast to await further orders.

Rumors from the north reached Greene's army in South Carolina. Washington was marching south to trap Cornwallis. The French fleet was bound for Chesapeake Bay to cut off British escape by sea. Some of the newer men wondered if a great victory might soon bring the war to an end. Few of the tough Maryland and Delaware veterans believed it.

Perhaps two hundred continentals remained of the fourteen hundred who had marched south with De Kalb in the early summer of 1780. They had faced the pride of the British army at Camden, Cowpens, Guilford Court House, Hobkirk's Hill, Eutaw Springs, and in countless nearly forgotten skirmishes. But each battle had only given way to more marching. Marching in cold rain and blazing sun, marching with bleeding feet and hungry bellies. Three thousand miles of marching back and forth across the Carolinas. The veterans settled themselves by their campfires. Let the new men waste the night talking of the end of the war. The veterans would rest while they had the chance. In the morning, there would no doubt be more marching. Perhaps some dreamed of peace—of an end to the fighting and marching—and smiled in their sleep at the thought.

General Lord Charles Cornwallis surrendered to General George Washington at Yorktown, Virginia, October 19, 1781. When the news reached London, Parliament voted to make peace with the United States. The formal treaty ending the American Revolution was signed September 3, 1783.

Suggested Reading

Busch, Noel F. *Winter Quarters.* New York: Liveright, 1974.

Chidsey, Donald. *The War in the South.* New York: Crown, 1969.

Coggins, Jack. *Ships and Seamen of the American Revolution.* Harrisburg, Pa.: Stackpole Books, 1969.

Ketchum, Richard, ed. *The Revolution.* New York: American Heritage, 1958.

McDowell, Bart. *The Revolutionary War.* Washington: National Geographic Society, 1967.

Middlekauff, Robert. *The Glorious Cause.* New York: Oxford University Press, 1982.

Ward, Christopher. *The War of the Revolution.* New York: Macmillan, 1952.

Wright, Esmond. *The Fire of Liberty.* New York: St. Martin's, 1983.

Index

Adams, John, 11, 13, 15, 16, 18

Alexander, William, 42, 44

Alfred, 50

Alliance, 51, 54

Approaches (trenches), 59

Arnold, Benedict, 25, 26, 66, 76

Augusta (GA), 58

Bemis Heights, 26

Bennington (VT), 17

Bonhomme Richard, 51–55

Boston (MA), 12–13

Brandywine, 18–22, 32

Briar Creek, 58

Brinton's Ford, 18, 20

Burgoyne, John, 17, 25, 26, 67

Camden, 64, 66–69, 70–72, 76, 78

Campbell, Archibald, 58

Chad's Ford, 18–20

Charleston (SC), 17, 56, 58, 61–63, 72

Charlotte (NC), 75

Chew House, 28

Civil war in South, 63–66, 89

Clinton, Henry, 39, 45, 58, 61–64, 68

Comb's Hill, 44

Continental Congress, 13, 23, 34

Continental navy, 49

Conyngham, Gustavus, 49

Cornwallis, Charles, 13, 18, 21, 41–42, 61, 68, 69, 71, 72,

75, 77, 78, 82–89, 90, 91
Countess of Scarborough, 51
Cowpens, 79, 83
Cross Creek (NC), 64

Dan River, 83–85
Declaration of Independence,
    13
De Kalb, Baron, 66–71, 91
Delaware River, 13, 15–17
D'Estaing, Comte, 46, 59,
    61
Drake, 50
(Le) Duc de Duras, 50–51

Elkton (MD), 17
End of the war, 90, 91
Englishtown (NJ), 41
Eutaw Springs, 89

Fairfield (CT), 48
Fayetteville (NC), 64
Ferguson, Patrick, 73–75
Foraging, 28–29, 34
Fort Mercer, 29
Fort Mifflin, 29
France, 32, 34, 39, 45–46, 48
Franklin, Benjamin, 31–34, 50
Freehold (NJ), 41
Freeman's Farm, 25, 26

Frigates, 49

Gates, Horatio, 25, 26, 66–67,
    68, 69, 71, 75, 77
Georgetown (SC), 64
Georgia, invasion of, 56–61, 64
Germantown (PA), 26–27, 32
Greene, Nathanael, 18, 20, 27,
    34, 40, 44, 75–78, 83–89,
    91
Grenadiers, 20, 61
Groton (CT), 48
"Guerillas," 66, 72
Guilford Court House, 84, 86,
    88, 89

Hillsboro (NC), 66–69, 71, 85
Hobkirk's Hill, 89
Hopkins, Esek, 49
Howard, John, 81, 82
Howe, William, 11, 13, 15, 17,
    18–19, 20, 22, 23, 28, 29,
    39, 41
Howe, Richard, 46
Hudson River Valley, 17, 25
Huger, Isaac, 83, 84

Jones, John Paul, 50–55

King's Mountain, 73–75
Knyphausen, William, 18–19,
    20, 22, 41

Lafayette, Marquis de, 22, 40, 66, 91
Landais, Pierre, 51, 54
Lee, Charles, 40–42, 45, 84, 85
Lee, Henry, 77
Leslie, Alexander, 78
Lexington (MA), 13
Lincoln, Benjamin, 58, 59, 61, 62, 63
Louis XVI, 33

Marie-Antoinette, 33
Marion, Francis, 66, 77
Mercenaries, 13
Monmouth Court House, 41, 43, 45
Moore's Creek Bridge (NC), 64
Morgan, Daniel, 76–79, 81–84
Morristown (NJ), 47, 65
Moultrie, William, 58

New Haven (CT), 48
New Jersey, 13, 16, 40
    See also Englishtown, Freehold, Morristown, Princeton, Trenton
New London (CT), 48
Newport (RI), 46, 56
New Providence (Bahamas), 49
New York City, 13, 15, 17, 39, 40, 46, 56, 65
Ninety-Six, 64, 72, 75, 77, 78

North Carolina, 56, 58, 72, 75, 86
    See also Charlotte, Fayetteville, Hillsboro, Moore's Creek Bridge, Ramsour's Mill
Norwalk (CT), 48
"No taxation without representation," 12

Old State House, 14
"Old Wagoner," 76, 79
Osborne's Hill, 20
"Over-mountain" men, 73

Pallas, 51, 54
Paoli Tavern, 23
Pearson, Richard, 52
Philadelphia (PA), 11–24
Pickens, Andrew, 66, 77, 79, 81, 82, 85
Pitcher, Molly, 43
Prevost, Augustine, 58
Princeton (NJ), 15
Privateer fleet, 48–49
Providence, 50
Providence (RI), 46
Pulaski, Casimir, 61

"Quarter," 65

Ramsour's Mill (NC), 82, 83

Ranger, 50
Reading Furnace, 23
Revenge, 49

Salisbury, 83, 84
Sandy Hollow, 20
Saratoga (NY), 26, 32, 67, 76
Savannah (GA), 58–61
Scarborough, 51, 54
Scottish Highland regulars, 81, 82
Serapis, 51–55
Seven Years' War, 12
Sorties (raids), 59
South Carolina, 56, 58, 63, 64, 89, 91
    See also Charleston, Georgetown
Stark, John, 17
Steuben, Baron von, 35–38, 40, 44, 91
Sullivan, John, 18, 19, 20, 26, 46
Sullivan's Island, 62
Sumpter, Thomas, 66, 77
Supplies, 29, 31, 34, 46, 49, 65, 66, 68, 84
"Swamp Fox," 66

Tarleton, Banastre, 64, 65, 68, 69, 77–83
"Tarleton's quarter," 64–65, 75
Tennessee frontiersmen, 73
Tories, 63–65, 72–73, 86, 89
Tory Legion, 64, 81
Trenton (NJ), 15

Valley Forge, 29–31, 34, 35, 40
Vengeance, 51
Virginia, 58; militia, 69, 73, 86, 87

Washington, George, 11, 13, 15, 16, 17, 18, 19, 20, 22, 23, 26, 28, 29, 31, 34, 35, 40, 41, 42, 44, 45, 46, 65, 76, 90, 91
Washington, William, 77–78
Wayne, Anthony, 20, 22, 23, 29, 40, 42, 44
White Marsh, 29
White Plains (NY), 46
Williams, Otho, 68, 69, 84, 85
Wilmington (DE), 18, 29
Winter quarters, 29, 30, 34, 47, 65

Yorktown surrender, 90, 91